Microsoft Office 365 2017 for Mac: An Easy Guide for Beginners

Copyright © 2017.

All rights reserved.
This book or any portion thereof may not be reproduced or used in any manner whatsoever without the express written permission of the publisher except for the use of brief quotations in a book review.

Microsoft has released another update to the Microsoft Office 365 suite of programs. This latest update for the Office suite is designed, as the initial versions, to meet the needs of Mac users in the professional, home or school spheres. Consequently, it has received rave reviews for its attention to the demands of the market. The updated Suite of programs include Microsoft Word, Microsoft PowerPoint, Microsoft Excel and Microsoft Outlook. This update is an enhanced version of the model released in July 2015 for the OS X software.

Microsoft PowerPoint in this version boasts an improved user interface, provides users with new and modern animation panes, Collaboration and the Threaded Comments feature that enables seamless integration of notations, pointers and slides. Microsoft Excel is designed to be compatible with the basic keyboard shortcuts. It also boasts features that include Analysis Toolpak and Pivot Table; both ideal for efficient analytical functions and filters. Microsoft Word continues to offer users updated ClipArt and editing options while the Outlook application offers users updated calendars, support for a Master Category list and new web-based archive support for its users.

Microsoft has advised that this of the Microsoft Office 365 version is compatible with several Mac computers. A few of the compatible Mac models include the Xserve, Mac Pro, Mac Mini, MacBook Pro, MacBook Air, iMac and the MacBook.

The purpose of this book is to explore the various applications included in the Microsoft Office 365 suite of applications. It will also provide details on how to best navigate and utilize all the new software brings to the table. It is hoped that at the end of the book, the wealth of knowledge surrounding the Microsoft Suite will be sufficiently enhanced to ensure maximum user experience.

1. Office for Mac
   The user can get started quickly with the updated versions of the usual Microsoft Office products. These include newer versions of Word,

Excel, PowerPoint, Outlook and OneNote. There will be a combination of the familiarity of the Office suite and the unique Mac features you are accustomed to.

2. Getting what you need done
   Easily find the feature you require in the Office suite. This will allow you to create documents quickly easily with many built-in automated design and research tools.

3. Collaboration
   Whether the user is the working online or offline, the collaborative effort is fully supported. The collaborative effort is done in real time on whatever you are doing.

Users will be facilitated to be able to give their input in whatever form they can one a single document.

4. Movement
   The platform will offer the user up to 1 TB of cloud storage for their documents. These documents will be readily accessible when you are ready for them. This completely facilitates the online collaborative environment so the user can continue working on something they were working on at an earlier time.

5. Office 365 Customers
   The Office 365 customers will be the first persons to access the

new Office for the platform. The user will have office applications on their Mac or PC, apps on the tablets and apps for the smartphones as well. For the other times, the Office Online access will be available when the user is on the go.

6. Office Blog
   A blog is a great way used to keep readers informed on topic. An Office blog will be no different as the user will be kept updated with new features or product news and so much more. When new items are released, the blog will be one of the first places that information can be found.

7. Quick Start Guide

The Quick Start Guide is a quick way for users to access the knowledge on how to complete a task easily. Since the applications are new versions, the quick start guide will give the user an introduction to these applications.

8. Support
   When a user is interacting with the platform they can access support as they need. They may have questions and needs and they can seek the answers they need. There are many popular topics with queries that would have been answered before. Therefore, the user can search these topics and find the previously posted answer to their concern.

9. Word
   Microsoft Word is the state of the art authoring tool that allows the user to create polished documents effortlessly. The new insights pane will show the relevant contextual information conveniently in the Word application. There is a Design tab that will enable the user to manage their colors, layouts and fonts across the documents.

10. Sharing and reviewing documents
    When users collaborate, it is believed that they can get more done in a quicker time frame. This is facilitated by working together with built in tools that are used to share and review documents. This can have

several persons working on the same documents simultaneously along with threaded comments beside the relevant text.

11.   Excel
Using Excel will allow the user of the software to turn their numbers into Insights. Using the familiar keyboard shortcuts, the user will have additional enhancements like autocomplete and the formula builder that will make you more productive.

12.   Visualizing data
Once data is entered in Excel, the software can help to visualize the data by using the recommended charts that will be best suited for the information.

Previews can also be done to see the different options that are available. With things, such as PivotTable Slicers, the user can help to discover patters in the larger data sets.

13. PowerPoint
PowerPoint will allow the user to create attractive presentations with greater confidence. There is a new Presenter view that will show the viewer the current slide, next slide, speaker notes and the timer on the Mac. The user will see this information while the presentation only will be projected to the big screen.

14. Animation Pane

There is an Animation Pane that will help to design and fine tune the animations and refine the transitions to ensure that there is a polished finished product. The presentation ca then be easily shared with others as desired or invite other users to work on the same presentation.

15. OneNote
    The ability to organize, capture and share ideas with the digital notebooks that can be accessed on any device. It contains a powerful search engine that can be used to track things such as tag, indexes along with the ability to recognize text in images and handwritten notes.

16. Formatting
Formats such as italicize, bold, underline and highlights can be added to the fonts that are placed in documents in Office 365. The user can format their notes in any way they desire. These notes can then be shared with family, friends or colleagues so all parties can work on tasks, projects or general plans.
17. Outlook
The user can use Outlook to manage their email, contacts, calendars and tasks in a much easier way. The new Outlook for Mac is equipped with push mail support so at all times the inbox will be up to date.
18. Conversation view

There has been an improved view that takes the form of a conversation which sorts the inbox of the user around threaded conversations. This will allow all the messages to be neatly organized so you can easily find them. There is also a new message preview that will give you the first line of an email just below the subject line.

19. Templates

The average user creating a document will want to get going in the shortest amount of time while still looking professional. Therefore, they now have an option to use over 1000 professionally designed templates to jumpstart their work. This will have users completing great looking documents in no time.

20. Sharper look
The documents and text that are viewed on the Mac will look sharper than ever. This is in relation to the Retina display that comes on the Mac computer which will enable your presentations or documents to look stunning.

21. Gestures
With the inclusion of gestures, the user can navigate their spreadsheets, documents and presentations seamlessly. The gestures will allow the user to make natural movements that are intuitive using their Multi-Touch gestures.

22. Ribbon Menu
There are many features that are intuitive and are contained in the Ribbon menu. These features are neatly organized in menus that users can easily find them. These are convenient options that can be used to enhance the document to produce the best results.

23. Integration
Office 365 offer integration with other applications that are useful to the user. Applications such as OneDrive, OneDrive for Business and SharePoint helps to increase the productivity of the user by adding functionality. Your files can be access on the Mac and other devices once you have

signed in with your Office identity.

24. Insights Pane
The Insights Pane contained within the Word application is powered by Bing. This powerful feature allows the user to access the contextual information from the internet within the document in real time.

25. Co-authoring
Many instances will call for collaborative effort on a document in which the finished product is a combination of creative energies. This is facilitated by Co-authoring which will enable several persons as enabled by you to work simultaneously on the same document. There

are also trackers to clearly identify who made what changes.

26.   Mail Merge
Mail merging is one of the powerful tasks that the user can use Microsoft Office 365 to complete for them. One thing that makes this exceptional is that it can use the combination of applications (i.e. Excel, Word and Outlook) to achieve this powerful tasks.

27.   Analysis Toolpak
It is important to note that the Excel application can do many complex calculations for the user. One of the areas that can be applied is the Analysis Toolpak that can be used to do various intricate

statistical or engineering analyses.

28. Windows sharing
One of the exceptional things that can now be done is the sharing of information with the Mac and the Windows systems. Many of the functions are supported for easier file sharing between the two platforms. This is a great improvement that allows the flexibility between multiple users to share information across platforms.

29. Themes
Themes can be applied to documents or presentations to give them an enhanced look. This can help the creator of the document to still produce amazing presentations while simply focusing on the

content. The Theme variants will allow the user to choose different color schemes for each theme that is applied.

30. Conflict Resolution
The conflict resolution will allow the user to visually compare any changes that have been made. This will allow them to see any changes that are causing a conflict and this will allow them to decide what version they would like to keep.

31. Capturing Notes
The user can capture their notes whenever they need to. There is no restriction to what you can capture including pictures, audio and even handwriting. The OneNote application can be the

digital notebook of the user.

32. Remain Organized
When the notes are made, the user can do various things including creating, moving, copying, reordering and renaming to keep their notes organized. They can also do things such as color coding, searching and deleting to be able to organize the content as you desire.

33. Online Archive
The user has the option to move email messages from their inbox to an Online Archive located on the server to make additional space in the mailbox. This online archive folder in the navigation pane provides

access to the archived messages when it is needed.

34. Proposing a new time
This feature allows the user when they receive a proposed meeting time that will not work for you, the system can propose a new meeting time. This will allow the meeting organizer to easily accept or decline the proposal. The system makes this a seamless process with minimal intervention by the user.

35. Multiple Calendars
The user may maintain multiple calendars for various reasons. One may be maintained for personal events and another for business related activities. The

Office 365 system will allow the user to look and maintain the multiple calendars as necessary. It is also important to note that there is a feature that allows the user to view the multiple calendars side by side.

36. Weather Forecast

The weather forecast can be provided right in the Calendar without the user having to leave the application. All the local forecasts will show the weather in the calendar view. It will be convenient to know what the weather will be wherever you are and even better you do not have to be distracted to go search for it.

37. Category Sync

The categories that are included in the Outlook application will be synced and this includes their names and their colors. They can be synced and this applies to all versions of Outlook, namely Outlook for Mac, Outlook for Windows and the Outlook Web App.

38.   Built in Assistance
The user of the software can stay focused on be more productive using the smarter ways to find the information of features they need. The Word Researcher can be used to find and use the content related to the topic without leaving Word. Things such as references, citations and images can be used to complete a solid draft.

39. Tell Me
The Tell Me feature can be used to find the right command that is needed at the time. All that is required is to type what you need to achieve and in the intelligent box the user can select the command to be executed.

40. Best Design
The designer features contained in the applications are an intelligent with a tool that will create very high quality slides in a short period. There is a new Morph transition that will create a cinematic transition between the slides.

41. Sway

The user will be able to share their dynamic presentations, reports or their personal stories with anyone. The Sway function will allow the user to add multimedia to an online canvas that will look amazing on any device.

42. Data trends
The Excel software allows the forecasting based on the current trends that are in the data. The forecast can be affected by things such as the history and seasonality. The complex data can come to life.

43. Keyboard
The Touch and inking capabilities will give the user the amazing option to review, edit or present.

44. Get from Start to Finish in Minutes
The Sway functionality will make it quick and easy to create dynamic content that will be professional looking. The personal stories can contain interactivity and with great content, that will complete the package.

45. Interactive Content
Your presentations can come to life by including interactive content. This can give greater insight to your document when it contains original dynamic content. An example of this is adding a video that talks about your different ideas or maybe an interactive chart that will allow users to

drill down into further details.

46. Suggested Search Results
The contained Sway feature will suggest searches to help the user find images, videos, tweets and other relevant content that you can drag and drop into your document. There is no longer a need to have multiple apps open to get something done effectively. Everything can be done conveniently in one place.

47. Office Lens
This is a new and innovative app that will allow the user to trim, enhance and make pictures of the white boards and your documents clear so they

can be easily read. When this is completed they can be saved to OneNote.

48. Delve
   This app can be useful in large organizations that produce a large about of content and you will need to find documents quickly. The Delve app can be used to discover, find and share these documents in the organization.

49. Skype
   The recognized Skype app is one that is associated with Microsoft 365. This is a convenient calling app that allows users to stay in touch with others using free video and voice calls. Messaging and file sharing is also included in this application.

50. Office for iOS
While using Office 365 on your Mac computer, the Office suite is also now available for your other iOS devices. This has made productivity easier as these apps have the similar look and feel of Microsoft office along with the touch experience.

CPSIA information can be obtained
at www.ICGtesting.com
Printed in the USA
BVHW040241140519
548207BV00011B/103/P

9 781542 508339